t h e c r a z y t h i n g t h e c r

g t h e c r a z y t h i n g t h e c

n g t h e c r a z y t h i n g t h e

i n g t h e c r a z y t h i n g t h e

n g t h e c r a z y t h i n g t h e

h i n g t h e c r a z y t h i n g t h

i n g t h e c r a z y t h i n g t h e

h i n g t h e c r a z y t h i n g t h

i n g t h e c r a z y t h i n g t h e

h i n g t h e c r a z y t h i n g t h

i n g t h e c r a z y t h i n g t h e

h i n g t h e c r a z y t h i n g t h

i n g t h e c r a z y t h i n g t h e

h i n g t h e c r a z y t h i n g t

t h i n g t h e c r a z y t h i n g

h t h i n g t h e c r a z y t h i n g

y t h i n g t h e c r a z y t h i n g

a y t h i n g t h e c r a z y t h i n

r a z y t h i n g t h e c r a z y t h i

*Before things began the Crazy Thing lay evenly distributed everywhere.*

*They
tried to corral
every iteration of
the Crazy Thing's
name, but one by one
the letters escaped,
refusing to spell
out anything.*

the crazy thing

When
angels wrote out
its name on the head
of a pin once too often,
the Crazy Thing struck a
match and lit the fuse. The
ensuing BANG rattled
windows and doors all
over the wide
universe.

the crazy thing the crazy thing the crazy thing the crazy thing th

thing the crazy thing the crazy thing the crazy thing the crazy th

thing the crazy thing the crazy thing the crazy thing the crazy

therazycrazy thithe crazy thing the crazy thing the crazy thing the crazy thing t
the crazy thing the crazy thing the crazy thing the crazy thing t
thing the crazy the crazy thing the crazy thing the crazy thing the crazy thing
thing the crazy thing the crazy thing the crazy thing the crazy t
thing the crazy thing the crazy thing the crazy thing the crazy thing the crazy t
thing the crazy thing the crazy thing the crazy thing the crazy
crazy thing the crazy thing the crazy thing the crazy thing the crazy thing the c
the crazy thing the crazy thing the crazy thing the crazy thing the c
the crazy thing the crazy t the crazy thing the crazy thing the crazy thing the crazy thing the c
thing the c the crazy thing the crazy thing the crazy thing the crazy thing the c
crazy thing the the crazy t the crazy thing the crazy thing the crazy thing the crazy thing the cr
crazy thing the crazy thing the crazy thing the crazy thing the cr
the crazy thing the crazy t the crazy thing the crazy thing the crazy thing the crazy thing the cr
the crazy thing the crazy thing the crazy thing the crazy thing the ci
thing the crazy thing the c the crazy thing the crazy thing the crazy thing the crazy thing the ci
thing the c the crazy thing the crazy thing the crazy thing the crazy thing the c
crazy thing the thing the c the crazy thing the crazy thing the crazy thing the crazy thing the cr
crazy thing the crazy thing the crazy thing the crazy thing the cr
crazy thing the the crazy t the crazy thing the crazy thing the crazy thing the crazy thing the ci
the crazy t the crazy thing the crazy thing the crazy thing the crazy thing the ci
the crazy thing thing the c the crazy thing the crazy thing the crazy thing the crazy thing the ci
thing the c the crazy thing the crazy thing the crazy thing the crazy thing the cr
thing the crazy crazy thing thing the crazy thing the crazy thing the crazy thing the crazy thing
the crazy t thing the crazy thing the crazy thing the crazy thing the crazy thing
crazy thing the the crazy t thing the crazy thing the crazy thing the crazy thing the crazy thing
thing the c thing the crazy thing the crazy thing the crazy thing the crazy thing
the crazy thing thing the c thing the crazy thing the crazy thing the crazy thing the crazy thing
thing the c thing the crazy thing the crazy thing the crazy thing the crazy thing
thing the crazy crazy thing thing the crazy thing the crazy thing the crazy thing the crazy thing
the crazy t thing the crazy thing the crazy thing the crazy thing the crazy thing
crazy thing the the crazy t thing the crazy thing the crazy thing the crazy thing the crazy thing
thing the c thing the crazy thing the crazy thing the crazy thing the crazy thing
crazy thing the thing the c thing the crazy thing the crazy thing the crazy thing the crazy thing
crazy thing thing the crazy thing the crazy thing the crazy thing the crazy thing
the crazy thing the crazy t thing the crazy thing the crazy thing the crazy thing the crazy thing
the crazy thing the crazy thing the crazy thing the crazy thing
thing the crazy thing the crazy thing the crazy thing the crazy thing the crazy t
thing the crazy thing the crazy thing the crazy thing the crazy th
crazy thing the thing the crazy thing the crazy thing the crazy thing the crazy
crazy thing the crazy thing the crazy thing the crazy thing the
the crazy thing the crazy thing the crazy thing the crazy thing the crazy thing th

the crazy thing the crazy thing the crazy thing the crazy thing th

the crazy thing the crazy thing the crazy thing the crazy thing th

thing the crazy thing the crazy thing the crazy thing the crazy thi

**Starting over from the beginning somewhere near the end**

THE CRAZY THING

**Carl Lehmann-Haupt**

**Codhill Press**

Deep gratitude to Lorraine Kisley, who planted the seed,
to Stephanie LaFarge and Enrique Zaldivar, who brought it
to fruition, to David Appelbaum, whose conversation has been
the seed bed from which it grew, and to my wife, who trimmed
and shaped its style over the many years of its writing.
Thanks also to Mark Matousek, who made me focus on the story,
and to Maria Longo, Dale Fuller, Betsy Carter,
Hoyt Hobbs, Hugh Delehanty, Roger Lipsey, Ken Krushel,
Kathryn Weld, Christopher Lehmann-Haupt, Preston Maybank,
Jane Grigorieff, and Sarah Smith.

Design and illustration by Carl Lehmann-Haupt

Library of Congress Cataloging-in-Publication Data

Lehmann-Haupt, Carl, author.
The crazy thing : Starting over from the beginning somewhere near
the end / Carl Lehmann-Haupt. -- First edition.
7 volumes cm
Includes bibliographical references and index.
ISBN 1-930337-79-5 (alk. paper)
1. Lehmann-Haupt, Carl. 2. Spiritual biography. I. Title.

BL73.L44A3 2014
204.092--dc23
[B]

2014026676

For Celestine Frost

*Compatriot of all the miracles of learning years*

Then their eyes will pop

sweating through their pupils,

And they'll remember

their yesterdays today

Like they didn't remember their

yesterdays yesterday.

# P R E A M B L E

"THAT'S A CRAZY THING you got there," the great Israeli composer Stefan Wolpe told his students whenever they brought him a composition he liked. He meant that it had a life in it that couldn't be explained because, one, it was crazy, and two, it came from a wild and crazy place.

I borrowed the phrase to describe moments in my everyday life when my mind is changed so radically and at the same time, so subtly, that though everything is altered, nothing is disturbed. All at once I know myself as part of a universe that contains things as near as forks and knives and as far away as the most distant galaxies. It's as though the world has become a single chord and I am trembling microscopically in sympathy with everything from sub-atomic particles and silvery sardines to the dusty surface of Mars. "This is a crazy thing," I say to myself, rubbing my eyes, because I feel as if I've woken from a dead man's dream.

This event, this change that changes nothing, is unmistakable when it occurs. I *could* say it's as if a great gong has

sounded, a bell I'm so close to I might be standing inside
it when the clapper claps and the sound waves ripple
through everything within earshot and beyond, but there
is no place in the experience for metaphors. Comparisons,
figures of speech, come after the fact. The event itself is
unqualifiable. In that immense instant, I understand the
difference between being someone — a person with a
name, an address, a family, and a job — and Being itself,
the Being of beings. I've been preoccupied with this knowledge all my life; it's the defining event that makes this auto-
biography (the writing of the self) possible. When it occurs
it's shocking; in a flash I learn that the world and I exist in
a continuum, I within the world and the world in me.

Given the singularity of this event, it's inexplicable to
me that I never notice the moment when I return to flat
land. My eyes have been opened and then they close.
I forget everything that has just been revealed to me. I
form a picture of what has happened to me: The picture
stands for the event, but it contains nothing of the
experience. Remembering the image, I forget the real di-
mensions of the self and then I forget that I have forgotten. Why? Why do I forget what I wish to remember, and
remember what I ought to forget?

"And what is it that you wish to remember?" a voice
in me will ask.

"Why the Crazy Thing of course!"

"And that is ... what, exactly?"

"TILT!" Warning lights go off. "DO NOT TRY TO
ANSWER THIS QUESTION!" No one can say what the

Crazy Thing is because it isn't anything. I call it crazy because it's so unpredictable, but I'm completely wrong to call it a thing. It is nameless, absent, sudden: from nowhere it slips in and plants its charge. By the time the detonation goes off, it's already gone.

Sixteen years ago I decided to write a book about these singular events. It was July, 1998. I was between jobs and we had moved south for the summer, down to the little cottage on James Island in South Carolina where C has always gone in July and August. The house belongs to her family, and it's called Fiddler's Green, in honor of the fiddler crabs that swarm in the marshes. I had found myself a place to work in a corner of the boathouse and every morning I went there to think about the impossible task I had set for myself. How could I write about something I couldn't picture or name? How could I even think about it?

Putting the question that way is misleading. It suggests a possible mastery, as if there were a technique that would open the doors to the event. What I wished was to enter a state of hovering anticipation that neither points nor grasps. I wanted to look without looking for anything in particular, and in this way make myself ready for whatever might happen.

I decided to go for a walk, a searching walk in which I actually sought nothing more than a state of attentive waiting. I called this waiting "looking for eternity," because, like the idea of eternity, it has no end. Eternity, being everywhere and nowhere at the same time, both hidden and exposed, is not something one can point to.

I would walk with the sole purpose of building up a posture of vigilance in myself. It was early in the morning when I set out. Roscoe the dog came too because he had seen me slip a green tennis ball into my pocket.

The house looked out on a tidal inlet and rumors of the sea were never far off. Long vees of pelicans patrolled the sound. The air was salty and the weather unpredictable. Interminable droughts could be interrupted by sudden squalls when the wind would rip through the leaves of the huge live oak in the driveway and rain would beat down insanely on the tin roof, and then, as suddenly, the sun would come out again and the only remaining evidence of the storm was the few drops of water dripping from the gutters. The hummingbird came back to the feeder. The lizards came out from under the sofa. Roscoe the dog came out from under the house. Once, lightning struck out of a clear June sky not twenty feet from where I was sitting. It banged so loud and suddenly I could think of nothing for a long time afterwards.

I held the screen door open as Roscoe picked his way down the stairs. There was nothing he loved more than chasing balls, and he did it with immaculate concentration. A few steps from the house I threw the ball as hard and high as I could. It bounced once. With flawless timing the dog left the ground, and, twisting as he leaped, snapped it out of the air. Then he trotted into the surf and flopped down, cooling his long underbelly in the waves while he waited for me to catch up. He wasn't looking for eternity; he was already there, living in some kind of timeless immediacy. When I think of Roscoe, lying now in the cool earth under the oak behind the house, I think of the sunny morning in June when I went out in search of eternity and he came too.

I headed for the back field where a stand of ancient pecans was slowly dying out. The sun dappled the grass about the trees. With earnest concentration I planted one foot on the ground and then the other. I heard the wood storks rise up from their roost in the pine trees, their wings drumming noisily. Across the wide water I could see the Morris Island lighthouse at the eastern end of Folly Beach. On the far side of Folly, the illimitable ocean beat on the shifting sands.

I turned my attention inward then, and made myself ready. I wanted to set up a sentinel in my mind, in a high place beyond where thoughts are always forming. I wanted to step away, to extricate myself from the trees and the ground, from the drone of the insects and the sharp piercing cries of the gulls. From that high place I meant to keep watch — on myself and on the landscape as it formed and reformed itself with each step. Round the pond I went and into the orchard where the earth was soft underfoot and colonies of fire ants dotted the field.

My attention is unstable at best, and never more so than when, in the spirit of self-observation, I turn it toward myself. Suddenly I think of all the things I forgot to do, but I know such thoughts have only one purpose — to distract me. So I interrupt them ... and interrupt them again and again each time they start up anew. With each interruption some awareness is gained: Now I'm conscious of my breath; then of my hearing; then my body comes to life, as if it too could think. I can feel the shock and shudder of my footsteps; I can smell the sweet exhalations of the oleanders mingling with the marshes' salty rot. As I work my way free of idle thoughts, a tall pillar of attention is growing that will soon reach beyond thinking. From this tall vantage point I'll be able to both see and be seen. Rounding a bend near the dock, a cardinal spots me from his place in the underbrush. His color is explosive. He is watching me from out of his extreme redness.

It's absurd to look for eternity. Where would something that huge hide — behind the tractor or among the rows of civvy beans? And wouldn't it blind anyone it ever appeared to? Eternity's essence may be stillness itself, but the best I can hope for is to catch flashes of it, as if eternity were a tinderbox or a powder keg.

My efforts to be vigilant kindle a spark in my brain; it smolders in my mind, flickers along a dendrite, leaps a synapse, and flares up. When I pay heed to the motion of walking from where it begins down low in my belly, other spots of intensity catch fire in succession: the soles of my feet as they press on the ground, the moving muscles in my abdomen and chest as they gather and distribute the air, the base of my throat, my brow and the back of my skull, and, at the end, a place just over my head where a wick would be if I were a candle.

As I walk the length of the dock, the flame is burning; it gutters when I turn, dies out, and flares up again as I step from the weathered boards back onto the earth. Now I feel as though I am in two places at once, both above myself and below, both inside and out. And then something hot burns into my mind. I try to catch it, but it tears through, shredding and singeing everything in its passage. The idea of eternity enters my mind like a burning meteorite. It's far too big and too hot to be contained; it bursts through the narrow bands of my thought and scatters the contents of my mind. Sheer delight springs up in my heart, and simultaneously, an unfathomable sorrow.

I am still walking. Once again I reach into my pocket and take out the tennis ball, bounce it once to get the dog's attention, then throw it hard. The ball arcs into the air and time stops. From this point on, events no longer succeed one another, but appear as sculptures in a frieze. I see all this in a vision: see my attention travel out along my arm and follow the ball. I see Roscoe racing toward the point he's calculated the ball will bounce. The dog is leaping to catch the ball; the sky is darkening; the branches of the cedar tree are bobbing up and down in the rising wind. A line is drawn from the soles of my feet into the upper air. The dog snatches the ball and comes down on all fours. He is turning toward me. He is coming toward me at a trot. An immensely tall thought has split the air — a scribble of lightning — and it stops me where I am, stops me and leaves me waiting, waiting expectantly for nothing, waiting without end.

In this way, on a day in June on James Island, South Carolina, I met eternity — and was left hanging. The idea of eternity scooped me out and left a hollow, a hankering, a hunger knot that will not go away and only grows and grows with the passing of time.

Friday, January 2, 2015   Before sending this initial segment of my book off to the printer I want to comment briefly on some peculiarities of its composition and publication.

*The Crazy Thing* is not a book for the general reader. I'm writing it (it is still under way) to my friends; that is, to those people who share my concern that I/we have not yet begun to live our real lives. We form an invisible brotherhood through the anguish of the shared question: Will we have learned to live by the time we come to the end?

The readers I address are those same forlorn insomniacs who think, as I do, that the only life worth living is the one spent in search of the elusive shape and stature of the self. But here's a caveat: by self I do not mean some private personal sense of my own identity that sets me off from others. I am not advocating a form of meditative withdrawal into private navel gazing. I've done plenty of that in my life, and I regret the wasted years. Under the sway of that illusion, I would never have learned what astonishing emotional intelligence is concealed in every person's heart.

Awakening, becoming what one essentially is, is an extra-personal process. The self one awakens to may be curved, fractured, erased, homemade, a-temporal, or polyphonic. But it can only be realized in relation to others. I can't do this alone. I need to work with and for other people, the ones we sometimes call neighbors, as well as that other within me —

the second nature in myself that is usually concealed. Enlightenment, knowledge of Being, is for everyone and it arises from All.

I've chosen to publish *The Crazy Thing* serially, rather than as a completed work, because I want to finish it in conversation with my friends. The small volume you are holding is the first in a series of eight. The subsequent seven volumes will become available as I complete them in the months to come. I have established a website — thecrazything.net — where the reader may post his or her comments, observations, questions, and refutations with the assurance that I will refer to those comments as I write the succeeding volumes. The writing of *The Crazy Thing* will be carried out in relation to the community it engenders.

Another peculiarity of the book is that while it is a memoir — a compilation of the memories of a single person — it is not only the past that is remembered. My aim is to find a way to remember the future — to provoke a future that is different from the one we are presently facing. To remember the future, to be present at the birth of that unqualifiable event that alters nothing while changing everything, requires vigilance. I cannot cause anything to happen directly, but with vigilance, the maintenance of an attitude of pure expectation, I can at least clear a space in which the unexpected might come to pass.

Early this morning, while it was still dark, I found myself surrendering to a revolutionary force, as if in obedience to a will not my own, but not belonging to any one else either. It's this gesture of surrender that I call "remembering the future" —a gesture that inevitably draws me into the community of those who also question, and without which a radically new future will never come to be.

# dIAGNOSIS

I WAS SITTING IN MY STUDY telling my friend S about the diagnosis — rogue cells in a lymph node just above the clavicle — a stage three tumor on the tonsil ... radiation ... radical dissection of the neck. I was talking very quickly and S, whom I have known since I was eighteen, had closed her eyes. When I paused, she opened them again and with extreme precision, planted her question:

*"If you had to die now, in what ways would it be too soon?"*

The conversation took place in the winter of 2003. I was sixty-five.

"We found a few malignant cells in a lymph node at the base of your throat," the ENT told me, his eyes skidding past mine and coming to rest on the wall behind me. I arranged a matter-of-fact expression on my face. I wanted to give the impression that I handled tough stuff like this every day. "Until we find the tumor," he went on, "the possibility of lung cancer can't be ruled out, though it's statistically unlikely. A PET scan should show us where it is. Once we know that, we'll know how to treat it." I willed my eyes to meet his as I stood up. It hadn't yet dawned on me that I was the person he was talking about.

On the taxi ride home, my driver got into an endless argument with a truck driver. I left the cab in a rage and jumped into another. I pushed some bills into the front seat and urged the new driver not to dawdle. Only when I was home and lying face down on my bed did I remember leaving my glasses in the first cab and my backpack in the second.

Three months before, I had been on the evening shuttle coming home from Washington, D.C. when I raised my hand to touch a sore spot on my neck and found a painful swelling the size of a marble. It was gone by morning, but C advised me to see my doctor anyway. Dr. L scribbled a name on a piece of paper. "It's probably nothing," she said, "but you should check it out with a specialist."

"And if it's not nothing?"

She paused a long second before she said, "Lymphoma."

Dr. P ordered a CT scan, and then another when the first showed only a slight thickening of the throat tissue. The second was as inconclusive as the first. "I don't see anything," he said, "but I'm troubled by what I don't see." This time he ordered a sonogram with a fine needle aspiration. It made me mad. "Cancer doesn't swell up and go away, does it?" I found myself wondering how much money he made each time he ordered a test. Six weeks later, as I was complaining to the lab technician administering the test, she interrupted me. "Loog," she said in her blunt, Slavic accent, "id's ubvious you god something. Don't you tink it would be better to know what?" When the doctor's office called a few days later to make an appointment, I yelled at the receptionist, "Why can't he tell me on the phone?"

Wednesday, May 5, 2013   Eight years have careened past; I'll be seventy-five this summer and a lot has changed since I lived in the lovely, ramshackle brownstone on East 93rd Street I shared with C for half a lifetime. I no longer commute to an office in Washington, D.C., or walk a couple of miles a day, or read aloud to my wife in the evening. Even the way I write has changed. Now memory emerges under the pressure of two silences — the one that came before and the other that's coming soon.

Twice a year I visit my oncologist. He runs a scope through my nose, sticks an inquiring finger down my throat, and, finding nothing, pats me on the shoulder: so far, so good.

Over these years I have assembled a large file of fragments — stories, shards of memories, bits of remembered conversations, dreams, letters, and the data from my experiments — from which I mean to compose a clearer picture of my life than the one I lived in the confusion of the everyday. As I arrange

these fragments into their new order, I will interrupt the story
they tell with occasional recent journal entries so that in the
end I will have written a double narrative in which the past and
present are juxtaposed.

   I've begun many things in my life. Most withered before
they could take hold, but a few put down roots and grew into
the central themes of my existence. I want to dig down to
those roots, water and feed and loosen the soil around them,
so that, by beginning over, I might cause them to flourish and
ripen into real maturity "somewhere near the end".


FOLLOWING MY DIAGNOSIS, I continued to go to the office. I had the PET
scan done in a New York lab on a Thursday and flew to
Washington the following Monday to review designs for
the upcoming issue of the magazine. In the general staff
meeting that began the week I felt like an invisible man.
The voices of people around me seemed to come from
very far away and when I spoke, it was as if through a
long tube. After the meeting, I slipped out of the building to call my doctor. He told me that the scan had
shown a stage three tumor in the left tonsil. They
would have to do a biopsy, then treat the tumor with
chemotherapy or radiation before doing a radical neck
dissection to remove the lymph nodes in the left neck
that could have been affected. I returned to the office
and told my boss, explaining that I would need to take a
six-month leave of absence. He seemed very affected by
the news, but I felt oddly relieved. At that moment I

understood how much it had cost me to fend off the thought of my own death. Now I no longer had to pretend that I was going to live forever.

That evening I rode the bike I kept in my office along the Potomac and stopped to rest on a bench by the boat basin before making the long climb up Rock Creek Parkway that would bring me to my hotel. I was filled with strange thoughts as I watched the last scull dock. The stars were coming out. At the far end of the bench a woman said something and it took me a minute before I realized she was talking to me. "Please forgive me," she said in heavily accented English. "I have come here from my home in Ecuador because my husband, a diplomat, was being treated in one of your hospitals. He died this afternoon." After a long pause she went on: "I will fly home in the morning. But I saw this spot from my window and it seemed so beautiful that I couldn't resist leaving my room for a little while to sit here. Then you came and you looked so quiet that I thought it might be permissible to speak to you. *Lo siento mucho.* I am sorry to trouble your evening."

I asked her about her husband, and her life in Ecuador, and we continued talking in this way for about half an hour. Later, as she walked away, I wondered whether she would have spoken so freely to me if I hadn't found out I had cancer that morning.

Friday, May 7, 2013  **A few years ago I went to a recital of late Beethoven sonatas. The pianist was good and I** listened with pleasure to the first half of the concert, but after the intermission, when he struck the urgent, opening chords of the Hammerklavier Sonata, something completely unexpected occurred. The dense music, alternately pounding and lyrical, called up the memory of a childhood landscape that I had completely forgotten. At first the thought was distracting and I tried to dismiss it, but the landscape kept recurring, and with it the feelings and sensations of the summer I turned fifteen, when I worked at a children's camp in New Hampshire teaching horseback riding. I had just begun to be aware of the great themes of living — love, religion, art, and philosophy — but in a completely inchoate way. The music was urgent and sublime, and in the same way a single note struck on the piano will set many others vibrating sympathetically, it stirred the memory of those obscure promptings I felt that long-ago year I carried a copy of *Walden* everywhere and had already begun to make paintings and woodcuts filled with portentous symbols. There were great thoughts and feelings moving blindly in my unformed mind. Sometimes, late at night, I went to sit under a tree in the middle of a field. The nights were clear and the field sloped down from the woods behind me to a line of trees below. Leaning against the tree, I could see mountains rising in the distance and the wide starry sky overhead.

The grandeur of the sonata led me back to that field — there was no escaping it — and then from the field to the tree and the tall grass I had sat in when, on a particular night in August, I saw a meteor rise up from behind the woods on my left and, moving in a stately and majestic manner, slowly burn its way across the entire night sky from one horizon to the other. I don't know how long it took to reach the far side, but it was time enough for me to feel how singular the event was, and, being a romantic kid, I took it to be a sign the heavens had made for me: my life would be special.

Later, when I understood that meteors can't possibly send signals to searching adolescents, I more or less forgot about it. In any case, my oracle was a vague one. It offered no stirring prediction that would set me on my path, nor any indication of the way my life might be special. But listening to Beethoven's sublime piano music nearly sixty years later, I began to understand the meaning of that adolescent dawning. There was more at stake in my recollection than I had realized.

My "oracle" was, in fact, prescient in that it printed an image of incommensurable vastness onto my imagination. That endless night sky was my first intuition of the possible scale of my mind and of the presence in it of the idea of the infinite. It marked me with an endless longing. For the rest of my life I would feel cramped in tight spaces. From that same claustrophobia grew the impulse to search for ways to exceed the limits of my understanding.

The high emotion of the Hammerklavier Sonata had rescued a powerful and misunderstood feeling from the crystallized oblivion we call remembering. Recalling the power of that event clarified the character of the task that lay before me. To know "in what ways it would be too soon to die," I needed to remember the turning points in my life, the beginnings of the several vocations for which I'm responsible. I'm writing in order to situate those points in a different temporal order than everyday time. There are no beginnings in everyday time: each day resembles the last. A narration with a beginning and end, a prophecy and its fulfillment, unfolds in an order of time that's different from everyday time. Only in this time does it matter if the augury is fulfilled. In my book I'm attempting to recast my story in this what might be called "heroic time." Only in heroic time could it be "too soon to die." Writing this book will guide me in this endeavor: It will teach me how to live (and die) or I will have failed as a writer.

RETURNING TO MY HOTEL that night I had dinner at the bar. When I went upstairs to my room, I fell asleep before I could get my socks off. The next morning while it was still dark I was shocked awake by a dream.

I had been standing in front of a café in a small French village talking with a beautiful young woman when I saw her eyes shift focus to something behind me. Turning, I saw a cool, dark figure in a pale blue jacket and fashionable short white linen trousers sauntering toward me across the square. He had one hand raised, as if to detain me, and instantly I recognized him. He was Death, come to collect my soul and lock it away in the specimen box he carried in his pocket.

Like a sprinter exploding from the blocks, I started for him with murderous intent. He turned and loped away on the points of his elegant shoes. Rage boiled up in me, growing as I ran, til it was high as a house, and the house on fire. Death dodged into a narrow lane and I pounded after him, through narrow streets, past shops and houses and up a long, winding staircase to a closed courtyard surrounded by an iron railing heavy with wisteria vines. In fury I charged him, meaning to tear his arms and eyelids off, but before I could get close to where he was calmly standing, he drew a long knife from the folds of his shirt and slipped its point between his own ribs. With a strange, ironic smile he collapsed at my feet.

I woke up panting, my heart pounding and my face flushed with triumph. I had defeated death! Then, gradually, as my labored breathing slowed, I realized I was not alone. The old wooden dresser at the foot of my bed seemed to have been waiting for me, as had the wrought iron lamp in the corner, and indeed every other object in the room. They were all waiting for me to show up. Together we turned toward the window and watched the first light break over the rooftops. This wasn't just any morning — it was morning on earth, morning in the solar system! The daybreak was vast, and though it looked no different from other mornings, it felt taller and wider than usual and it came from farther away.

Thursday, May 9, 2013 **When I was nineteen I thought about killing myself every day. It was the darkest year of my life. I was living in a fifth-floor walk-up on 108th Street in New York City, had few friends, and spent any free time I had with my nose in a book. The only people I talked to were the editors, designers, and space salesmen I saw in the office of a** trade magazine where my job was to distribute mail several times a day. Four nights a week I went to classes at Columbia's School of General Studies, and on Saturdays and Sundays I worked all day at Carpenter Library. Twice a week I went to see a psychotherapist, with no apparent effect. Every night, as I closed my eyes, I promised myself I would do it the next day.

I went downtown to Abercrombie & Fitch to buy a gun. In those days it was a haberdashery for wealthy commuters from Westchester and Fairfield Counties. Rifles and shotguns were displayed in glass cases on the second floor. I squinted to see the large numbers written on tiny price tags hanging by a thread from the trigger guards. When the sales clerk offered his help, I waved him off. Finding the cheapest one, I thought: "I could pay for this one with my savings, but if I changed my mind, where would I find the money for next semester's tuition?" Apparently I wanted to go on living, although at the time I couldn't imagine a life different from the cramped, alien, lonely one I'd decided not to end.

In my despair, I had hardly noticed that at that darkest moment when I thought I might want to take my life, my real story — or stories — began: I fell in love with a beautiful poet; I met a man who made me think I might be an artist; and I was introduced to the teaching that would engage me for the rest of my life.

C WENT WITH ME to meet the palliative care doctor. He didn't mince words. "Cancer treatment is like medieval torture. You are going to suffer. We'll take out that tonsil and you'll have thirty-seven radiation treatments, followed by a radical neck dissection to remove any affected lymph nodes. The cancer won't kill you, but you'll have a dry mouth, bad teeth, and skewed taste buds for the rest of your life. And no more drinking."

"Not even a glass of wine at dinner?" I asked.

"You can have two glasses of wine a year — one on your birthday and the other on New Year's.

"You'll also need a peg. That's a tube inserted in your stomach so you can feed yourself when you can't swallow solid food anymore." He wasn't amused when I asked if I could mix a glass of burgundy in with the six cans of nutrient I'd inject into my stomach every day. Instead he offered me a vial of liquid Vicodin.

Would I be cured at the end?

"You're never cured of cancer. It can always come back."

I went down to the radiation lab in the basement where I had to lie on a white table in the middle of a large, bare room while a technician tattooed a blue spot on my neck. Then I was fitted with a mesh mask that would be bolted to the table during the treatment. With my head locked down, the radiation machine could beam a stream of protons along the same three angles every day. Someone had painted an autumn landscape on the ceiling for patients to gaze at while the machine buzzed at them: I got fifteen seconds to the left neck, fifteen to the right, and thirty in front. It didn't matter — in fact it helped — that the painting was so clumsy.

I saw a skinny guy with a bright red neck in the dressing room and the look in his eyes was sad and hopeless. His despair scared me and I told myself that no matter how badly things turned out, I would find some way to resist that degree of gloom.

In late December, a surgeon with the cleanest glasses I'd ever seen took out my left tonsil; a few days later, another put the peg in my stomach. In early January, I began treatment. The radiation glanced off the gold in my teeth, singeing my tongue and burning my throat. After a week I bit into a banana and it tasted like an acid sponge. From then on I ate no more solid food, injecting instead a viscous nutrient into my stomach every afternoon. After another week the nurse practitioner told me to stop talking. "Anything above a whisper could permanently damage your vocal cords," she explained. C was already getting hard of hearing. When she couldn't hear my whisper, I scribbled words on a yellow pad. When she couldn't read my scrawl, I would sometimes lose my temper.

A few weeks after my treatments began, C was diagnosed with breast cancer. "Now I've got it," she said angrily as she came into my study. She hadn't told me when they'd found a lump in her breast, but the biopsy confirmed what the doctor already suspected. It was my turn to care for her — to accompany her to all her appointments and tests. She was scheduled for a mastectomy the following week. I held her hand in the recovery room as she came out of the anesthesia before dashing off to my own treatment. It would have been funny, except, of course, it wasn't.

She was dressed and ready when I came to take her home the next day, standing in the middle of the room with the drains still hanging from her shoulder, reprimanding the internist's secretary because she hadn't sent papers over for her release. The operation was a success. She would require no chemo or radiation. That evening she went out to the park for her walk with the dog.

Three weeks of radiation brought me to the breaking point. Pain kept me awake for hours at night and sometimes I was so constipated I couldn't sit down. To distract myself, I read through a complete set of Georges Simenon mysteries and when I was too tired to read I worked on building a model of a trawler, mindlessly sanding tiny pieces of balsawood in the small hours of the morning and gluing them into place. These activities diverted me, but they didn't cure me of the temptation to feel sorry for myself.

Friday, May 19, 2013   "Every night," C says with a note of defiance, "I ask God in French, English, Latin, and classical Greek, to give us our daily bread, and to forgive us our sins, and not to lead us into temptation but deliver us from evil." It was as if she were asserting, in her polyglot way, the right to revert to the simple practices of her childhood. "And then, as I lay me down to sleep," she went on, "I ask God to bless everyone I know or ever knew, starting with you and Jane and Preston and Whitaker …" Here I interrupted her, because I knew she would cheerfully go on enumerating all upon whom the Lord should cast His blessing, "right down to the tiniest molecule," as she likes to say, and I wanted to start dinner.

She is changing. It's not just the creeping loss of short-term memory. She has become simpler and more direct. She isn't interested in complicated ideas; she doesn't want to write sad poetry about death or having Alzheimer's. But she is fierce in her dedication to all her old practices. She does an hour of yoga twice a day, swims and trains with weights three times a week, and walks every day in the park. She always keeps a notebook by her side at night, and writes blindly in it in the dark or in the early morning when she's still half asleep. In this way she harvests what she calls "givens", the dreams and odd sentences she hears between sleeping and waking. Every morning she types them up and shows them to me. Most are disconnected bits and pieces, but some come charged with so much poetry and wit, they cry out for the whole poem from which they appear to have been detached.

> *At ninety-nine*
> *Ariel demands*
> *That you think cross-diamond*
> *& Allegory galore*

Sometimes we work together on these particles, and I find that, with little or no prompting, she can assemble them into moving and coherent poems — as if my interest provided the necessary motivation to carry out what she couldn't quite do by herself.

IN TIMES OF CONFUSION or doubt, otherwise rational people will sometimes visit a fortuneteller or open a favorite book to a randomly-chosen paragraph, in hopes of finding an answer to whatever knotty problem is troubling them. I go to an art museum. When I had reached the point in my treatment when I could no longer speak above a whisper or remember what real food tasted like, I realized I was in danger of falling prey to dark thoughts and despair. So I took myself to the Metropolitan Museum and began to wander from room to room, on the lookout for a painting that might offer me a way out of the enclosing darkness. At the back of the Lehmann Collection I came upon Vuillard's *Interior with a Figure*, and for reasons that are now obscure to me, I gave myself up to the study of this painting.

The figure in question is the painter's mother and she's sitting by a window on the far side of the room, mending a white comforter. But the real subject of the painting is the play of light: over the wallpaper, the lace curtains at the window, and the round table with the red and black tablecloth in the foreground.

I follow a certain ritual when I look at a painting. With half my attention I let my eyes roam freely from one

painterly event to another; with the other, I attend to the
events they trigger in my viscera. For this Vuillard, it was
the way a happy conjunction of pinks and browns
produced warmth in the region of my heart, how the
relation of red tones in the tablecloth caused my ears to
glow, or how the progression of the painter's brush
strokes across the ceiling started a tom-tom of anticipation in my throat. The white cloth had gathered a charge
of light into itself that it released in small increments, so
that reflections bounced off the ceiling, dissolving color
and eating away at the solid legs of the table til they appeared as thin as needles. When I practice this indirect
way of looking, I see a painting I might have missed. The
table in the foreground, as big and round as a bass drum,
appears to be chortling. Its laughter is derisive. It laughs
because Madame Vuillard completely ignores the
riotous performance of light and pattern that's playing
out around her. Nor do any of the people in Vuillard's
paintings take note of their surroundings. They read
newspapers, write letters, flirt, dream, and doze, oblivious to the crazy patterns, layered one upon another, that
are the events of this painter's art.

Studying one of Vuillard's paintings gave me a way of
looking, or rather gazing, at my surroundings that leaves
no time or space for despair. At the first sign of a dark
mood, I'll look around my room and begin counting the
steps the light makes as it enters the window and is
reflected from one surface to another — bright at the
window frame and darker by degrees as it reaches into

the shadows under the desk and behind the radiator. It is as if I am mentally painting my room. Instead of a random pattern of light, I begin to see a scale of tones — do, re, mi — with which I will make my composition. But I don't stop with my room. When I look out the window I now see the sky itself as a luminary that softens the harsh glare of the sunlight and distributes a larger scale of tones over the landscape. Watching the changes at dawn, the landscape of rooftops, extends the practice. Sometimes I take it one step further and make a leap into spaces I can only imagine. I picture a sunrise on Jupiter's moons or a rainbow on Venus and I try to link these imagined events to the dappled patterns of the leaves on my wall.

And my bad mood yields. Despair vanishes in that flood of light, to be replaced by an altogether different mode of thinking and feeling — as different from where I began as sunlight is from the dark, destructive light coming from the radiation machine.

Thursday, May 30, 2013  **Now, with all my heart, I call to mind as vividly as I can my two friends, D and G, with whom I spent the day yesterday. I had left the house while it was still dark, so that I was already waiting in the long morning shadows just outside the Pelham Park subway station when G stopped her car in front of me and opened the door, greeting me with her lovely low voice even as I touched my cheek to hers and pulled the seatbelt across my chest.**

I summon her now (as I do the philosopher we were going to visit a two-hour drive away) as I might summon a tutelary spirit or a hidden god. For it is when I am in intimate conversation with both of them that I am able to feel the substance of time in a way so palpable and pure that it admits no admixture of space, or distance, or absence.

We had each expressed a wish to see one another one last time before we went our separate summer ways. We volunteered, G and I, to drive to the philosopher's barn-red house in the woods this time, since it is usually he who comes from so far away to meet us in the city, in that darkened room with its book-lined walls where we gather each Wednesday night all during the scholastic year. And now, sitting at lunch on the back porch, waving a wasp away from the cheese, I look around at the others' faces and am struck, perhaps for the first time, by the power of our association. It is a subtle gift that has allowed us, in the company of two or three others, to work together week after week for almost ten years now, and to be both surprised and surprising each time we spend an hour together, exploring the resources of our collective attention. Left alone, none of us could come close to the rarified vision we can summon together, an ability to see into the deep structure of the world. I had always thought this vision was the gift we offered each other, and although partially true, it strikes me now that our friendship is the real gift.

Only after we had moved outside onto the porch for lunch, had the philosopher, in his precise way, asked about the nature of this gift: "While we are separate people, as different as we can be in our professions and marriages, how does it happen that when we are together we set each other free from the bondage to our personalities we experience in almost every other condition? You are a dancer and teacher of Vedic philosophy," he said, turning to G, "and you an artist or designer, or whatever it was that you used to do before you began to write this crazy book you've put us in. I am a philosopher. But these facts, and many other features of our persons, fall away when we work together. It is as if we become strangers to each other when we meet, but strangers who are strangely familiar, as if indeed we were one stranger, or one host. And if this is true," D continued, "it raises a further question: Can we, when we are apart, offer each other this same enabling gift?"

It was this question that allowed me, on the morning of the following day, even before I began to write, to "summon them with all my heart," these two friends I had spent the previous day with. Finding the careful effort to imagine them enables me to enter a mode of solitude and silence that is closed to me when I'm alone and not engaged in speaking with these friends.

I WAS GIVEN A COUPLE of weeks to recover from the radiation before the surgeon with the very clean glasses opened the left side of my neck and took out sixty-four lymph nodes. The operation took much longer than he had predicted, and when he emerged eight hours later, C was sure it was to tell her that I'd died. Instead he led her into the recovery room, warning her that I might not recognize her at first. "Do you know who this is?" Dr. K asked me. "That's my wife," I whispered emphatically.

I spent the night in the intensive care unit, hooked up to every imaginable monitoring device: a sequential pressure machine massaged my legs continuously to prevent clotting and I was fed intravenously and emptied through a catheter. There were tiny flickering lights and little beeps sounding high and low as the oxygen in my blood rose and fell. Half awake and half asleep I waited for a dawn that seemed never to come. But all through that long night I was filled with a rare delight. Happiness is not the word for it, though I was strangely happy. I felt close to life, more intimately alive than I was used to being, and in love with every detail of my condition — the nurses, the machinery, the patients in their beds, and the comforting dark all filled me with an unaccustomed and fragile delight precisely because I had been in such close proximity to death.

Saturday, June 1, 2013  When I spoke with D this morning I asked him what he'd been thinking about. "Forgetting," he said. "I'm trying to understand forgetting." It turned out that he meant something very dark by this, oblivion so complete that one is no longer aware that anything has been lost. And yet what's gone is everything that's most precious — affections, values, honor, love, the gifts, as it were, of the spirit. What remains is the ego that remembers things only as they pertain to its blind sovereignty.

I was shocked. I'd spent a lifetime studying ways to resurrect a forgotten form of consciousness that changes the perception of even commonplace things into privileged moments, yet it had never occurred to me to ask about the oblivion that conceals them. It is memory itself, I learned, that harbors the subtlest forms of forgetting.

The duplicity of memory, its empty performance, is exposed when I experience a moment of involuntary remembering. The smell of wood burning so vividly recalls a favorite aunt's stone house in the Cevennes region of France that although, even after fifty years, I could draw the floor plan of that house, I have no single recollection of the time I spent there that can compare with the lively tone of my aunt's British inflections as she called "à table," when breakfast was ready, and the sweet sorrow that wrings my heart when I think of her, that comes back to me when I inhale the slightly acrid odor of wood burning in a fireplace. The Proustian recollection is proof that my past is alive in my unconscious. Why does it depend on accidental odors and tastes to be recalled, but otherwise lies dormant? Has anyone ever studied the subtle process of forgetting that robs me of my past — the reverse side of recall?

# dEATH & COMPANY

I DIDN'T WANT TO FORGET the urgency that my close brush with death had afforded me. Six months after I was diagnosed with cancer I went back to work. Under the hammering routine, the shock began to fade, and gradually the old, fatal complacency returned. I realized I wanted to know exactly what is lost when I lose the knowledge of my death.

So I began to practice for a short while every day, imagining that I could die that very moment — fall down on the sidewalk, slump over in my seat, strangle on a bit of food in a coffee shop — and leave life. I began almost exactly a year after I first found out I had cancer, in November of 2003, and I worked at it for about a month, keeping a daily record of how the thought of dying could still shock me awake. I chose the following entries from the mass of notes I kept at the time because I think they convey some of the surprise I felt at how edifying the conversation with death could still be.

Monday, November 7, 2004  **From the narrow alcove where I lie drinking my morning coffee I see the lamp in the corner grow pale as the first light of day begins. My chair by the window is empty; this is how it will be when I'm gone. All the familiar objects — the pencil-filled cup, the empty glass and scraps of paper on the windowsill — come to life in a way they never can when I'm in an ordinary state of mind. In my imagined absence, the simple objects of everyday use recover the natural dignity my everyday consciousness denies them.**

Thursday, November 10, 2004  **Tried today to imagine, not that I was going to die but that I could. Like meteors glancing off the earth's atmosphere, the thoughts of dying skid off me. I have plans, and dying is not among them. Next week my stepdaughter and her children are coming to town. Tonight for dinner I'm going to make roast pork.**

Sunday, November 1, 2004  **Walking down Lexington Avenue I tried to hold the death-thought in my mind and found that I couldn't. But when I held it in my body, it steadied me. It was as though I divided a very complicated number into itself and obtained one.**

Wednesday, November 16, 2004  **It is difficult to receive the thought of dying with grace. When I do, it is like putting down a heavy suitcase.**

Monday, November 21, 2004  **Any other thought is preferable to the thought of dying. Errant thoughts distract**

[34]

me ceaselessly. Yet when I regard these wandering thoughts as if they were nothing more than the buzzing of flies, courage seeps in. Now I'm ready, perfectly balanced on the balls of my feet and able to parry any distractions. There's no encounter I can't handle, including Mr. Death.

Wednesday, November 23, 2004  The death-thought is scorching; there is no attitude or pose that can stand up to it. It dries up all tears; it incinerates anxiety. When I need to know something accurately and beyond any doubt, I spend an hour with Death. Then I know that I exist. "I" appears in its absolute, irreducible validity. There is no more peerless companion than Death.

Friday, November 25, 2004  Yesterday I sat down on the bus and found myself facing two small children, probably sisters, possibly twins. They had turned round in their seats to watch a tiny barking dog being carried in its owner's arms to a seat further back in the bus. Their mother sat facing forward until one of them looked me squarely in the eyes and observed: "You're old. You're going to die soon!" Then, before their mortified mother could silence her, the other added, "Your teeth are so yellow." Speechless with delight, I tried to reassure the mother, but before I could find my words, the first girl added comfortingly — "I like your teeth. I just wish they weren't so yellow."

Tuesday, November 29, 2004  On the flight home last Wednesday I wondered how I could prepare for a possible crash. Regrets flooded my mind — so many things not done or done wrong. "This could get bad," I thought. "I'll need to be vigilant now."

So I began to gather patience and, bit by bit, like a boxer shaking himself awake when he hears the count nearing ten, I came to. Instead of feeling pulled down by the force of gravity, I was suspended, held up by the same lift that kept the plane aloft. Then I knew I was safe. Even if the plane went down in flames no harm could come to me. For a time I rested in this metaphysical safety, and then, as I walked through the terminal, it faded like a dream.

Thursday, December 1, 2004  The death-thought comes unbidden now. Last night when I opened the medicine chest, the death-thought fell out on me like a safe falling from a window. This afternoon, as I was trying to dislodge a bit of orange from between my teeth, it engulfed me. I melted like a piece of ice in front of an open furnace.

Sunday, December 4, 2004  It's time to change my death practice. This way is too heavy and too dire. I need a discipline that respects the delicate tracery of passing time. As I leave the subway station, I stop to listen. I hear the train departing and the steady beat of the turnstiles as the passengers leave. It slows as the last of them files out and disappears into the night.

There is dying in every instant. The conversation I had with a friend today will never be repeated. Things gather and then disperse, like seeds broadcast in the wind.

The denial of death is numbing. But when I know for certain that I can disappear at any moment, it frees me from dullness. Each instant becomes a possible starting point for something I have never done or said before. The thought of dying opens a passage that, like the straight gate of the gospels, leads directly to a life of such transfiguring intensity, I feel as if I had risen from the dead.

# ORIGINS

I WAS NEARLY SIXTY when I decided to write this book. In February 1998, we flew to Los Angeles to visit C's son for a few days. We slept on a mattress on the floor of his study and that first morning, still on East Coast time, I woke early to the sound of birdsong coming through the open window. The scent of lemon blossoms filled the air. It was as though we had flown from winter into spring. I was reading a book I'd begun on the plane when all at once, in the midst of reading, I suddenly decided to become a writer. It wasn't a whim. I decided, irrevocably, to write a book. The decision was absurd since I'd never written anything. I'd spent most of my life as a visual artist; even writing letters was difficult for me.

The book I'd been reading was Kierkegaard's *Purity of Heart* and it troubled me. It seemed to me that Kierkegaard was offering more than an idea to his reader. He seemed to be saying that if I'd read him in the right way, it would change the way I live.

I took him at his word. I decided to engage with him, read as he asked, and see if I could learn what he meant by "willing one thing". (That is the full title: *Purity of Heart Is to Will One Thing.*) Could reading Kierkegaard cure me of what he calls "double-mindedness"? I decided to read his book as if it were an instruction manual, follow his promptings, and write a book about my experience. I would call it *A Conversation with Kierkegaard.* I thought I could complete it in about a year.

Back home in New York, it was winter. The streets were frozen, and my project seemed far more difficult than I had anticipated. Months passed before I managed to write my first valid sentences.

*Now more than anything I want to tell you something. Now before it ends I urgently wish to speak. And I hope for words that are not empty, words whose fullness will be confirmed in the echo, in the answering conversation they evoke about each one's fundamental enterprise — to beat the devil, to establish oneself in the service of true speech, to answer, "I am here," when called.*

I typed out these words in a passion. For weeks I had been destroying everything I wrote. Now, in frustration, I spelled out my dilemma, and tasted, for the first time, the urgency with which I wished to write. The idea of writing what I already knew made me heartsick. Rather than report what I had discovered, I wanted, as I wrote, to discover what I was reporting. The simultaneity of knowing and speaking has everything to do with what Kierkegaard means by "willing one thing." A kind of violence is called for, one that can shatter the complacency of indifferent knowing and break through to the burning urgency of what needs to be said in the very instant of its saying. Years would go by before I began to understand what I'd discovered in that moment.

I stopped painting and began to write every day. I worked in the early morning dark before leaving the house, and in planes and trains, hotel rooms and vacation houses. I wrote one version of an opening chapter after another. Several months of hopeful work would result in a possible beginning, but when I sat down to read it later, my heart would sink. I knew it was bad. Nonetheless the following day would find me ready to start again.

Years went by in this way. I scribbled away furiously, filling notebooks while I searched in different ways for what it was I so urgently wished to say. I hadn't realized how much I would need to develop before I could give voice to the inchoate experience I wanted to write about — the mysterious other side of consciousness that only appears in fissures and in flashes. I hadn't yet seen that I didn't know how to think or write about it. I hadn't yet realized how shallow my understanding was. All I knew was that I had a blind need to give voice to something and that it wouldn't leave me in peace. The pages piled up and, with rare exceptions, were never quite to the point.

Then cancer intervened. I took it as a warning, a gun pointed at my temple, as if throat cancer were a cancer

of the voice and my instructions were precise: Speak,
write, say what you have to say or lose voice and life
both. The question about dying marked the opening
of the late, second stage of my life: I began to live
experimentally.

I continued to give myself assignments. I would learn
to walk or listen more consciously. I practiced daily, kept
notes, and then wrote up an account of my experiences.
In this way my book became more like an account ledger
or a kind of balance sheet that told me where I stood,
how much I'd paid, and what I still owed. Unwittingly, I
had given it the authority to teach, make demands, and
point out where I fell short. It directed me back to the
problem that Kierkegaard was speaking about in *Purity
of Heart*. Purged of double-mindedness, what would it
mean to will one thing?

It should be clear that Kierkegaard means something
more radical than doing one thing at a time. For the pure
at heart, consciousness, will, and action comprise a
seamless whole. In willing one thing there can be no gap
between myself and what I will — no ulterior motive, no
fingers crossed behind my back, and nothing left over.
It scarcely matters what I might do, because subject and
object, the will and the deed, should now be one. If I
were making a drawing, every touch of the pencil to the
page would complete something; both the drawing and
myself would be whole in every instant. Cézanne, for
whom beginning and end were indistinguishable,
worked that way. There are watercolors consisting of

only a few strokes that are completely satisfying, while even his most finished works are still "in progress."

Near the end of *Purity of Heart*, Kierkegaard questions his reader: "Do you now live so that you are conscious of yourself as an individual; that in each of your relations in which you come in touch with the outside world, you are conscious of yourself, and that at the same time you are related to yourself as an individual?"

No, the answer was certainly no. When I came in touch with the outside world I was not conscious of myself. I knew from many years of practice what it meant to be aware of myself, but that only came in flashes and was commonly lost when I entered into everyday relations with the world. I wanted to learn what it was that made me forget what I valued most.

Kierkegaard didn't say, "You must become aware of yourself." He questioned without commanding. His question invited me to question myself. When I asked myself if I was aware of myself, I became conscious of a hollow feeling, the absence in myself of something that should be there — the "I" was missing. I was a verb without a subject.

But the philosopher was subtle. His question made me aware that I was not aware — in other words, his question made me aware of myself. It was this initial exchange that put me on the path of writing. I wanted to write a book that would play Kierkegaard's part, take the role of midwife by posing subtle questions. It was the only way I could think of to learn what I couldn't or wouldn't teach myself.

Thursday, August 22, 2013  Meditative thinking is an oxymoron: I am supposed to keep still and keep moving at the same time; pay unbroken attention to my thoughts as they break up and reform; and wait without changing anything by so much as a hair's breadth for a change that will alter my nature absolutely.

This morning everything is the same as yesterday — an airplane drones by overhead, the shrimp flash in the glassy surface of the creek, and the children sleep late. But today an inner world is opening in which these events find an echo of unfathomable depth.

Another mind is moving in me, a second nature that is as inseparable from me as my shadow, except that in relation to it I am the shadow and it the light. The dilemma I find myself in (if I find myself at all) is that this other is hidden from me in the same way that seeing is hidden from things that are seen. The work of meditative thinking is a collaboration between these two natures — the seer that remembers and the seen that always forgets.  As in rowing, if you pull more on one oar than the other,  you go round in circles, and, as in rowing, all I can see is what I have passed as I press forward toward a point that is hidden behind me.

# Practicing

FOR CLOSE TO HALF A CENTURY I sat in silence every morning, and then one day I stopped. I was nineteen when I first heard of G. I. Gurdjieff's teaching, and, after moving to Paris in 1961, I began to study with one of his pupils. It was here that I learned the first steps, and I have been working on those themes ever since. Sitting quietly, practicing ways of developing one's attention for thirty or forty minutes every morning, is one of the central rituals of the teaching. There are others of course, and I'll speak of those in due time, but right now I want to say something about this miraculous opening practice that I struggled with for forty years and then gave up, only taking it up again now, almost a decade later, and this time with rather a different understanding.

Day after day I wrestled with wandering thoughts, cultivated the sensation of the different parts of my body until they came together in a single, resonant whole, followed my breathing attentively until I could feel a sensible charge entering with each inhalation. In the course of thirty or forty minutes I became filled with a rare and intelligent substance. Then I opened my eyes, got up from my chair to go about my business, and the jar containing that precious fluid tipped. What I had so carefully collected spilled out, and I returned again to my former rule of disorder and self-interest, the vision of the whole lost as detail after detail rose up to claim my weakened attention. The process, which had seemed sheer miracle when I began, grew repetitious by the end. Nonetheless I continued to follow the teaching, but only half believed in it. I began to read philosophy, study Tai Chi, and see a psychotherapist. Did I really know what I had given up? "Gurdjieff's is a great teaching with terrible students" was the way one man put it. Can terrible students really know the scope of the teaching they follow?

Later, old age came to unscrew my brains and drive spikes into my joints; the imminence of death was shocking. The list of insults to C's health alone would break anyone's heart: depression, followed by a series of psychotic episodes when she was in her thirties; then later, strokes, fractured bones, coronary arrhythmia — a fragile homeostasis that is maintained by as many as nine different pills a day. Two years ago, just before we decamped for Fiddler's Green, her family house on James Island where she's spent every summer since birth, she was diagnosed with Alzheimer's disease. In shock, in grief, in fear, in mourning, I began to sit again in the morning and found that now my mind opened at the point it used to stop. I realized I had been an indifferent student of a subtle and deep teaching and I decided to begin again, with a different premise.

Thursday, June 5, 2013  Spiritual teachers speak of silence as the beginning and end of all meditative practices. This would be uncontroversial if only one kind of silence existed. But there's another, and while one is golden, opening doors that too much talk keeps shut, the other is leaden, muzzling speech and suppressing natural questioning. The first is liberating while the other is an instrument of domination and repression. It often happens that the same teacher advocates both. He advocates the first in meditation exercises because a quiet mind serves as a portal to another quality of consciousness, but, being human, he also outlaws certain kinds of speech that might challenge his authority.

Only the pupil endowed with a critical mind can obtain the benefit of the first without falling prey to the second. As for the rest of us, years can go by before we understand the difference.

When in silence I withdraw from the chronic flow of inner talking in myself, a freeing power of insight is momentarily bestowed; I can see in two directions at once. I see my absorption — in an opinion, a dislike, or a reaction — and in that instant I also see behind me a wealth of feeling and intelligence that had been occluded by my limpet-like attachment to my opinions and judgments. If I persevere in this work of disengagement, the silence spreads and the things I see are now felt in the innermost chambers of my heart. The silence isn't mute. In it I hear voices that desire to find expression, as if another mind than mine were trying to speak through me, but with words too huge to emerge. Each syllable is the size of a boulder and each sentence as long as a mountain range. The rare person who can translate this more-than-human speech is able to evoke that procreative silence in others.

The way of silence is a dark path and leads through all the darkness of the human race. To arrive at actual silence, one has to pass through that night and see for oneself the role that cruelty, ambition, self-interest, and indifference play in our everyday lives. Though one shrinks from it, it is, in the end, a healing journey.

I formed a group with my philosopher friend, D — a group of two that grew in time to number six. I wanted to rethink silence and attempt to articulate the voices I heard speaking in it, an impossible task since the voice that my friend calls "the other" is untranslatable, at least in the impoverished vocabulary of contemporary speech. But I couldn't accept the standard solution, which is to pretend that the experience I'm looking for is ineffable and can only be expressed with the same handful of clichés that spiritually-inclined people pass down from one generation to another. I gave myself permission to speak nonsense in our group, in the hope that some of it might turn out to make sense in the end.

So I keep a notebook at my side when I sit and search, not for silence, but for the electrifying proximity of language that exceeds my understanding. There is a holy mystery that circulates, and it bestows its gifts according to a logic all its own. My prayers are vain; my will, inoperative. And yet, when the green maiden sings in my ear, the air is charged and I am overwhelmed by an encompassing softness. Reverence erupts in my heart; and suddenly I'm free because I'm able to suspend the sovereignty of my will.

The presence of others is enabling, so I meet with my colleagues each week. As we sit together in a circle, the façade of each one's personality almost instantly falls away. We are exposed: six candles blowing in the wind, six deep wells of meaning, six voice boxes giving approximate utterances to a deep and abiding mystery.

WHEN, AFTER A LAPSE of something like ten years, I resumed the practice of sitting in the morning, it was to inaugurate a new inquiry, one that didn't rely on any of the techniques of meditation I had been taught in the past. For years I had tried to bring about a change in my state. Special ways of sensing the body, breathing, counting, etc, can produce real and palpable alterations in one's awareness, and they prove that change is possible. But such efforts produce the illusion of a threshold, a doorway to a different way of being. Over and over I would find myself on the edge of a mode of feeling and thinking infinitely more intense and subtle than the ones I ordinarily experience. But I could never pass through. Inevitably I would fall back into my old ways.

In fact, the change I imagined was a will o' the wisp. I will never be free of the old man. My habits of mind, my illusions about myself, will persist to the end. What I can sometimes establish is a different relation to my flaws — my irritable nature, my arrogance, my hysteria — a relation of bare observation that thrives on impressions of my everyday self just as it is.

I call this practice "sitting." There is no technique involved in it. All I ask of myself is to sit still a bit longer than is comfortable, trying without trying to observe the events in my mind as they arise and pass away. There is nothing I can do to make this happen except to watch and wait. Each time I try to produce a known outcome, the very effort contradicts my search for an enduring passivity. In the search for pure receptivity, there is no method or technique beyond this one of taking note. Sometimes I try afterwards to give an account of what has happened. Then I learn something about the impossible difficulty of writing about an inner practice.

"I come face to face with my foe on a bare stone stage," I wrote one morning. "He's known by many names and there is no end to the number of different shapes he'll assume before I'm done — becoming in turn a spider, the odor of mint, an incurable disease, three notes sung by a bird, etc. Only my rectitude, my stillness, and my breath, will carry me past these distractions. Each inhalation makes me more sensitive to the event of presence. Now distant worlds move through my mind; galaxies course through my bloodstream. I adjust my stance, move my feet in preparation for what's coming next, and, in a single swift motion, I'm thrown to the ground. When I come to again, starlight is falling like rain. For a short while there is goodness in my heart."

"I got up this morning and went to my chair," I wrote on another occasion. "It was as if I'd been prompted: skip breakfast, skip coffee, sit down and be still. 'It doesn't matter if you wish for this or not,' it said. Vigilance is called for. If I perform the rite dutifully, it will free me from my personal motivations. So I sat for half an hour, and after a time I began to hum an open vowel. I pitched it to the hollow places in my chest, in my throat, in my abdomen and bowels. Ten minutes later it was as if another person were singing. A floating illusion (myself) has been replaced by a stable man: his feet are on the ground; his eyes are open. From somewhere out in space, a fiery understanding slaps me awake — I am not this; I am not that; I am."

A week later I noted: "Heavy going this morning. The mind is masterful in its power to fascinate. It draws my eyes to every object while it blinds me to what I'm looking for. It regales me with mean facts, plays on my resentments, or suggests I'm in danger. Like a despotic government, it rules by playing continually on my fears, and in this way keeps me dependent on it. How else can I explain the chronic anxiety that separates me everywhere from my heart's desire."

"This morning it's completely different," I reported some time later. "I ask myself what I want. I put the question deeply, as if addressing a disenfranchised population living in utter darkness. 'Longing' was the word that came back, as if from the bottom of a well, longing for longing. Then I surrendered to desire, and it carried me outward toward the sky. In a state of deep reverence I hear a beautiful voice intone the words: 'Responsibility for the sky,' over and over."

Sunday, May 9, 2013   If everyone in the human community has forgotten something, something that no one can remember and name, is it right to even speak about forgetting? Yet a conviction is growing in me that humans have forgotten something they could once remember.

When I speak about forgetting in this way, I'm not referring to the common variety everyone knows about, when I slap my forehead and say, "damn." I can recover from that kind of forgetting. The forgetting I'm talking about is an oblivion as inescapable as quicksand: the harder one struggles, the deeper one sinks. There is no cure for it. But I need to know it's there, accompanying me everywhere — a flaw in my vision of the world.

All around us we have evidence of progress — our growing mastery over nature, the exploration of space, medical advances, the conquest of disease, and so on. At the same time people speak of a forgotten relationship to the world — to brother wolf, to the ancestral dead, to time, to being, to the sky, to the gods — an intuitive relation grounded in feeling. But this way of naming what's been forgotten doesn't bring that world back any more than it can recall the affective experience on which it was founded. We need to begin with the question about forgetting itself. But the question itself is subject to constant erosion: Can I even remember to ask it, and then ask it again when I perceive that it has slipped out of my ken?

"WE HAD THE MOST extraordinary meeting last night," I told my wife, as I sat down in her wheelchair. C was confined to bed with a fractured pelvis.

"What did you say?" she asked, screwing a hearing aid into her left ear.

"We - had - an - extraordinary - meeting - last - night," I repeated slowly.

"You always say that, but you never tell me what you mean."

"I wish I could," I said.

"Try," she said.

"It's that we came to such a breadth of vision that I felt as if we were sitting on a balcony in heaven, looking out over the whole, wide creation. Of course we started in a far humbler place. But even at the beginning, something exceptional was moving among us. It began when one person said: 'I feel some very palpable influence coming from you all. In your company I can attend as I never do when I'm alone.'"

C was scribbling on the back of an envelope. It's the only way she can remember the things that attract her attention. Then the home health aide came in with breakfast, so it was early afternoon before we continued the conversation. C was drawing when I came back into the bedroom. I told her how I had found her aide in the kitchen, singing to herself as she read her tiny Bible, and how on a whim I'd asked her to repeat the exact line she'd been reading when I walked in. 'When He ascended up on high,' she read, 'He led captivity captive.' "It's from St. Paul," she said, citing chapter and verse.

"It was, in a way, what we were talking about in last night's meeting," I went on. "Someone spoke about the way her attention gets taken, captured really, by stray thoughts. And another person said that she was interested in what happened then, 'on the other side of distraction,' as she put it." C was scribbling again. "That was the opening that would lead us, at the end, to 'the balcony in heaven.' Why a balcony, I can't say. It's just the kind of image that comes to mind when one is in a very exalted state."

"Why opening?" C asked, still writing. And I went on talking for a while, trying to explain what I didn't know how to explain.

Later that night she read back to me what she'd heard: "You spoke about generosity of spirit, friendship, the ascent ... the edifying of the body in love. The recovery of a lost stature ... It makes me wish I could have been a fly on the wall," she said.

"Well C is a poet," I said to myself, "and she can hear things in my words that I myself am deaf to."

Wednesday, May 29, 2013  I hadn't drawn in years, not since I began to write this book, when someone showed me a drawing application for the iPhone and I quickly became addicted. Now I draw in the subway, in doctors' waiting rooms, and when, on my bike rides in the park, I stop off at the tennis courts to draw the players. I began to feel how much I had sacrificed to write this book.

Last night I made a drawing of C on my iPad and it wasn't half bad. Over the years my portraits of C had become a family joke. "Another drawing of his beloved," C would say in gentle mockery as I handed over the horrible scribble I had just completed. I hadn't been able to draw my wife, and after many attempts I gave up. Not only does this one look like her, but it's a good drawing, too. What does it mean that I can now take her portrait?

# 1EARNING TO WALK

I HAD HEARD OF A PERSON who celebrated his recovery from cancer by walking to California, and it made me think about what I could do to mark what I would call, with only a little irony, my second birth. During my recovery, while high on Vicodin, I imagined carrying out extravagant gestures: rowing a small boat around Manhattan and finding myself in the wake of a tugboat under the Brooklyn Bridge as the sun came up, or walking all the way to the high western desert to keep an all-night vigil there, watching the lightning dance over the steel rods at Walter de Maria's Lightning Fields. But as I knew I could scarcely walk to the far side of Central Park, I tried to think more soberly of what would constitute a pilgrimage for an old man with bad legs who wanted to live differently in the extra time he had been given. Putting together the two ideas, a pilgrimage and a new beginning, I decided to study walking, as if there were an art of walking that would be to ordinary ambulation as high cuisine is to take-out food.

My wife could hardly contain herself when I told her: "Learn to walk? Why your feet hardly touch the ground!" And she did a little hopping, jumping, cakewalk strut with an imaginary cane that made me see how droll my project seemed to her. It was something I'd been told several times before by my teachers: "You must learn to walk with your feet on the ground."

There were queer things that came to my attention as I began my apprenticeship, curious impressions that made me realize how little I knew myself. For example, there was the hairless monkey, or perhaps it was a boy — I wasn't sure which — who sometimes visited my imagination when I paid attention to walking. Quick and lithe as a natural athlete, this homunculus disported itself in my mind with the lightness and force of a fighter showing off his dexterity, but looked, to my eyes, strangely distorted. I took it to be the image of a separate, athletic intelligence that guided my movements without my conscious participation. I had to acknowledge that the distortion was in my mind, for the elf was graceful and self-possessed in all the ways that I wasn't. I felt his presence as I walked and he lent an odd independence to my movements. Even back in my study, when I was typing or turning the pages of a book, the gnome was there, guiding my fingers over the keyboard, scratching my ankle, or pinching the book's pages open as I read. I discovered that I was not alone; my body had its own mind. As I became more familiar with its wit, the grotesque image faded. But I didn't forget that there were two of us when I went walking. Now my task was to attune myself to this other. The joining of two minds, the mental and the moving, was the point of departure for a whole series of singular experiences.

When I look out my window at people crossing the street, everyone seems oblivious of the sidewalk. Is it only boxers, tightrope walkers, mimes, ballerinas, and martial artists who take an interest in the way their feet meet the ground? Not even my wife's teasing put me off. In fact I found it encouraging to think of myself as the least qualified candidate for prize walker. I already knew from my standing meditations that the relationship between my feet and the ground represented a new frontier of knowledge.

There's a stretch of sidewalk that runs along Fifth Avenue, between 90th and 96th Streets, where I went to practice every day. Among the small hexagonal paving stones that compose its surface, there isn't one that's level with its neighbor. A century of rain and frost has heaved them this way and that, and the roots of great elms have thrust them up in ridges. From across the street the surface looks flat enough, but up close I could see how it dipped, sloped, climbed, and tipped — the perfect place to study attentive walking.

It's hard to inhabit the unmediated experience of walking. Most of my movements have grown habitual, repeated so often they no longer require my conscious participation. I walk from room to room, lift my coffee cup to my lips, slice cucumbers, or run for the bus, and at night I move my mouth and tongue for an hour doing the different voices in the novel I'm reading to my wife. But can I remember whether I was sitting or standing when I brushed my teeth, or exactly how I disposed myself to cross the street in the middle of the block with the cars rushing past in both directions?

Does it even matter? I don't know what the circulation of my blood feels like and I'm none the worse for it. Why should I want to know what it feels like to walk? After all, it's usually only when I withdraw into a desert-like solitude that I can entertain the burning question that has become my passion — how can I learn to bring my attention to the boiling point again, so that everything I gaze on bears the halo of its singularity? The point of learning to walk, and more particularly to walk among other people, would be to shake myself awake from my complicity with the poisonous, average, leveling kind of awareness I agree to each time I come in contact with the world.

I began my study on a May morning in 2008. The stock market had crashed and I'd lost my job. Now every morning I was free to practice walking. It rained almost every day that month and the rain slipped off the leaves of the elms along Fifth Avenue and fell with a slap on my hat as I walked. I'd leave the house a little after six each morning, turn up 92nd Street, and head toward the stretch of sidewalk bordering the park that I'd chosen for my proving ground. Even before I got there I was preparing: I'd flex my knees a little, scuff my shoes on the rough sidewalk, and weigh myself first on one foot and then the other. Imagining a sheet of paper balanced on the crown of my head helped me hold myself erect, and this in turn permitted me a freer circulation of impressions between my feet and head.

But even my careful preparation was no defense against distractions. I'd be lucky to get as far as the corner before I'd forget about my experiment, and sometimes I'd only remember it again when I was nearing the park. I could deal with distractions when I sat. What was it about movement and the passing people that made it so hard to stay on task? When I got to Thorvaldsen Park, I always sat on a bench for a moment to gather my attention again, and only then would I turn down Fifth Avenue, walking very slowly and attentively, as far as the Engineer's Gate at 90th Street. Gradually I acquired a taste for simple walking.

Thursday, June 6, 2013 I looked around at my colleagues: the architect on my right, the plumber next to him, the philosopher across from me, and the yoga teacher on my left. "The distance I feel from each of you is shocking," I said. "I thought I knew you but I must have been dreaming. In the absence of that easy familiarity, I now feel how much attention I owe each of you. When I attend to you, I become attentive in a way I never can when I'm alone. It's not that I have the same

care for my neighbor as I have for myself; rather I attend to
myself to the degree that I first attend to my neighbor."


I WOULD EXPERIMENT for half an hour each morning, then come home
and write up my observations. In an entry from early
May I asked myself whether it's better to plant my feet
squarely on the sidewalk or let them fall on the ground
like a marionette's. Later that week I wrote instructions
to myself: trace the shock of your footfall as it passes up
the chalk pile — heel bone, ankle bone, radial and ulna,
femur, pelvis, and so forth until you can feel how each
step makes your ears jiggle. I felt like a radio with its dial
stuck between two stations called body and mind. It
was all static until I tuned my mind to the inner sensation
of my body. Then I got: "clear signal, better balance,
brighter mind."

I walked every day for weeks, and then months. Intelligence grew up where there had been none. When the
sidewalk got crowded I slipped through the moving mass
of pedestrians like a pickpocket — light-fingered, slip-
pery, quick-eyed. I saw the tree as well as its leaves; when
I looked at the ground I saw blades of grass, cigarette
butts, gum wrappers, and bits of broken glass — all in
sharp focus and all at the same time. The eye doesn't ordinarily work that way — my mind had grown quicker.

Events clustered. I saw a man stand on one leg to look
at the bottom of his shoe, even as a doorman whistled
for a cab and a pigeon strutted out between two cars.

These were trivial events, but because I was attuned, I saw them in counterpoint — chaos became polyphony and I entered the complex music of the world.

At first it was only my senses that were extended. From far away I could rake the stone wall edging the park with my fingertips. The sidewalk bristled with energy and I walked through it as I would tall grass. I could stroke tree bark, dog fur, and the silk of a lady's dress with my eyes, and from passersby I could breathe the odor of their moods as distinctly as if they had been cheeses — some as mild as goat, others as pissant as limburger. But as I reached further into myself, I discovered the hidden depths that lay concealed and unfathomed in the people I crossed.

An uncanny presence joined me each time I went out walking in this way. It began as an intimate feeling in the region of my solar plexus and then increased, filling me up til I brimmed with it, and then it passed beyond me, striding out ahead on its much longer legs and continued to grow until I couldn't keep up anymore. Just before it dissolved completely into the immensity of the air, it seemed to turn and say: "Follow me."

I always came back home to more conventional realities. I took the elevator to our floor, greeted my wife in her room by pulling her toes, read the paper, and scuffled with e-mail. Only when I wrote up my impressions of that day's walk would I begin to speculate. How is it that sometimes when I extended my leg it felt as hollow as a bubble and the surrounding air was solid. Am I sound and substantial flesh or filled with empty air like a balloon? At other times I could feel how I belonged to a sensitive field so wide and tall that its full extent went well beyond my mental grasp. Where do I come to an end and where does the world begin? The wider my mind grew, the more I shrank, until my social, civic self would simply vanish in the hugeness. Who is this incommensurably greater "I" who sometimes joins me, and then feels closer to me than I am to myself?

Through my walking practice, I had found an opening, a tiny porthole no bigger than my thumb. Through it I could see an amazing fire.

Tuesday, May 28, 2013   **No one told me when I was growing up that I would have to give an account of my life at the end. It was only holy rollers and *New Yorker* magazine cartoons that pictured a day of judgment. The clouds, St. Peter, and the Devil are figures from an old language. So what shall I call the imperative I now feel to justify my life?**

**I'd like to present myself as a seeker, one making claims for certain forgotten human possibilities. But as I too have mostly forgotten them, it's rather as a penitent seeker that I come. I have two natures — one is standing on the lower rungs of a ladder; the other somewhat higher. In those privileged moments when I know myself in the full measure of the self's stature, it is this higher other who knows me.**

# tHE CRAZY THING ITSELF

ALL MY LIFE I HAVE experienced moments of sudden, unexpected change. An excess of energy is revealed that strikes me dumb. Ordinary objects look noble — a milk carton acquires sudden dignity; friends are strangely trans-figured. And I myself feel like a statue that a revolu-tionary mob has toppled. Deposed from my imaginary pedestal, I look around and find I'm part of everything I see. Unnerved but relieved, I say to myself — "This is a crazy thing."

The Crazy Thing is always going away. Its departure leaves everything as it is, but changed. Imagine a huge maple tree in the middle of a field. A flight of starlings descends on it at evening, circles it once, and disappears into its leaves. The tree looks just as it did before the birds came — but now it is inhabited. Hundreds of wings, eyes, claws, beaks, and tongues live invisibly among the leaves. For one night the tree is home to the spirit of flight, to avian libido and avian philosophy. Something like this happens when the unnamable turbulence I call the Crazy Thing intervenes.

When it withdraws, it leaves me with a hankering, a yearning like the madness of love. I want to tell everyone about it, even the bus driver. But what can I say? The Crazy Thing is gone with the wind. High overhead I can hear it sweeping the world clean. If I tried to describe it directly, my page would be blank.

I was no more than three or four when it marked me. It was the end of summer and I was standing with my parents and older brother in the living room of our country house. The windows were shuttered and the suitcases had been loaded into the car. An hour before, the sky had turned yellow and the sound of distant thunder stole up the valley. Violent flashes of lightning danced on the treetops. The view across the river vanished in the mist; sudden gusts of rain raked the shingles of the roof like buckshot. And then a bolt of lightning hit the old oak that towered over the house. A huge limb crashed down on the roof beam, as if a giant had stomped right on it. The house shuddered and the ground shook. My parents turned pale and my brother started to cry. But I was laughing. I ran from room to room in wild, exultant glee. It was my first encounter with the Crazy Thing and it put its thumb on my forehead and marked me forever with a love for its excess.

In the beginning, the Crazy Thing often hovered around my infant consciousness; when I grew up, it withdrew to the edges of the world. Even before I left home, I had begun looking for it. Rumors of its passage, often false, were passed along to me. When I got to the place it was said to be, there were sometimes dust motes still swirling in the air, but the Crazy Thing was gone. I followed the rumors elsewhere. I crossed my own trail so often that it began to look like a child's scribble in a book, practically obliterating the text beneath. Eventually it dawned on me that I was following a siren song, an ever-receding thing. The closest I ever got to its exciting presence would be a place that it had recently swept clean.

All my life I have searched for the Crazy Thing. But how can I even look for something that can't be named and whose essential nature can never be known?

Monday, November 25, 2013  When I moved in with C in the fall of 1973, I hadn't seen the inside of her house for several years. Its appearance had changed a lot since her divorce. The children were off at boarding school and most of the antique furniture was gone. Now two dead bushes stood like candelabra at either end of the mantelpiece. A long sequence of drawings, most of them of a naked young man slumped out in a heroin coma, were taped high and low on the walls of the parlor, and the dining room was filled with stuff she'd hauled home from the park, notably a casket-shaped box that held a dented trumpet with no mouthpiece and a collection of twigs, leaves, branches, and weather-worn bits of

graphic ephemera. Up on the third floor, among the accumu-
lated junk that old families carry with them from generation
to generation, was an envelope that contained a lock of hair
that was said to be Lafayette's. And on every mirror in the
house C had scotch taped a piece of paper smaller than a fortune cookie's fortune, on which she'd typed a quotation from
Thoreau: "The perception of beauty is a moral test."

I didn't know at the time how precarious her situation was.
More than a year before, she had said goodbye to her husband
as she put him in a taxi on the corner of Lexington Avenue and,
dropping the last half-empty pack of her two-pack-a-day habit
in the trash bin, she walked, very slowly, back to a house that
was henceforth hers to live in as she saw fit. My arrival some
fifteen months later was part of a larger design: her aim was
to establish a home for creative artists that was also stable
enough in appearance for her to retain custody of her children.
Thoreau's claim that the ability to perceive beauty was tied up
somehow with morality was central to her understanding.
Living in a creative environment would be good for every
member of the family. A few years later her sixteen-year-old
daughter called the house "a mansion of good feeling."

We lived there for thirty-five years, and it nearly broke our
hearts to sell it. We ended up living in an apartment, a few
blocks away, which proved to be a good thing when C was
diagnosed with Alzheimer's disease three years ago. Because
she knew the neighborhood so well, she has been able to
maintain most of her familiar routines: she goes to the park
every day as she has for decades. And she continues to visit
the health club and the art school without confusion.

Nonetheless, she has changed.  A borderline depressive all her life, she's now resolutely cheerful. She still reads the newspaper from cover to cover, seeking out stories of natural disasters and personal misfortune as she always did, but now when you ask her how she's feeling, she replies: "Just dandy!" And small talk is hard. I can no longer ask her where she's been or who she's talked to, because she can't remember. Even if she could, her hearing is so compromised that I would have to put my question slowly, word by word, with careful enunciation, to make myself heard. I don't know which is worse: the grinding difficulty of daily communication or the growing silence and isolation that is gradually swallowing up my miraculous companion.

So sometimes we bark or moo or make up long chants and little ditties, or repeat the punch lines of old jokes, or imitate the voices of people long dead (C's a wicked mimic) just to make sounds at each other, and find that consoling. But when we sit quietly together I can feel her silent presence more strongly than I ever could when we used to make small talk about the day's events — proof to me that there is another part of her mind, perhaps a separate mind entirely, that is untouched by dementia.

I receive news of that second nature almost every day when she comes in from the bedroom to take her morning medications. Taking her pills in my presence, so that we both know she's had them, has become one of our rituals. Once that's done, she hands me her laptop and I read that morning's harvest. (We've both been at work for several hours by the time she comes in for our pill ritual — I in upright mode at my desk; she curled up and half-asleep with ballpoint in hand, listening for her givens, the overheard phrases and sentences of a voice she's taken dictation from all her life. She types them onto her laptop before she gets up.) Although she stopped writing poetry more than a decade ago, she has never stopped writing down her givens. They are gifts after all — perhaps supernatural ones — that she can't refuse. As long as I've known C, she's been the servant of that voice. All of her poetry first appeared as some combination of those givens. I had never been permitted to read any of them until, some months after her diagnosis, she began showing them to me.

I was astonished by what I read. The voice of the givens is very different from the superficial cockiness of C's everyday voice. It's as though I've been offered a window into her real feelings. It shocked (and relieved) me to discover this lucid witness to her inner life at the very moment that my sweet companion was disappearing. Among the things she typed out every morning were the very sentiments her daytime voice occluded.

> *My timetable is for the best*
> *It's not 101 Suicide*
>
> *Though at the right moment*
> *It aches in that direction.*

If I ask her what these lines mean to her, she shrugs and smiles helplessly. If I ask her to speculate, she's mute. She simply isn't able to question herself in the way she could in the past.

It's perhaps this very condition that permits the voices she hears to declare themselves so intelligibly.

I began taking an avid interest in these missives-from-elsewhere. Working together, we even made several complete poems by pasting up lines C had received over a period of several days. Her hand was sure. She knew just where the lines should break, and although she couldn't comment on their meaning, she was a certain judge of their quality. "What do you think of it?" I asked, about one of these assembled poems I was particularly pleased with. "It's okay," she said.

With the growth of my interest in C's givens, their frequency increased. They began arriving in broad daylight, while she was sitting on the toilet or walking in the park. When she complained about their sheer volume, I suggested she ignore some of them. "I can't do that," she said. "They're given to me by God."

No day brought the same style or quality of writing, and even within a single day there were many tones of voice, some profound and some that were only cracking wise. Sometimes whole poems came that required no editing at all. In late December, two such arrived, and both described her state more lucidly than she or I ever could. They convinced me that the poet lived on in her, whole and intact, and that the poet knew exactly how things stood.

The first was called "Lobotomy."

*And they removed one half*
*But left the other*

*A chick pea*
*With which I'll dream*
*To a conclusion*
*In the thorough night.*

*The other half was Grief*
*And as I've said before*
*I'll smile*

*Let Death pick His vague ramp*
*Let Death outrun our Opinion*
*Our*
*Dumped Woman*
*Doorstop*

A clue to the meaning of "doorstop" came in a poem called "Touchstone" that arrived a few days later.

*And keep the door open back to you*
*It's a crystal pool*
*and if you slip in*
*cool deep*
*and sink down*
*until your toe*
*can touch*
*the stone*
*you'll have learned*
*the work of life.*

*But the pool is bottomless* ———

*So how can you reach Heaven?*
*The golden apple is*
*in the pool*
*cold clear*
*dark*
*deep*
*And*
*if you can just … touch*
*it with your toe*
*you'll enter the*
*Vast*
*Kingdom*

*Just keep the door*
*to you*
*open*

The doorstop of the first poem is a portal to the vast kingdom in the other, because that is what even a "dumped woman doorstop" does — it keeps the door open.

An event like this one gives me pause: it makes me wonder about the role C plays, both in my life and in this book. It's as though she and I were two sides of a curious equation: she can speak powerfully and accurately without understanding what she's saying, while I struggle impotently to say what I'm consciously experiencing.

I always thought I knew what C had meant by taping Thoreau's words to the mirrors in the house where we'd lived together for so many years. But one day I tried to test that understanding by taking a long look at myself in the narrow, antique preening mirror that hung in the hallway. I found to my surprise that each time I looked, it was always with the same unspoken question: "Mirror, mirror, on the wall…." The mirror felt so far away, and my eyes had to travel so far out of my head to ask, that I never noticed how unconscious I'd become of Thoreau's words. All I could hear was my own perennial anxiety asking: "Am I the fairest in the land?"

With my question, the glass was empty; I could see no one reflected in its shining surface. But when, with effort, I called my eyes back to me, so that as I looked, I became conscious of myself as an individual — then the glass filled up. A strange, ethical beauty appeared when my vain, petty self was mirrored in the eyes of the other that I also am. I saw myself and smiled. The eyes in the mirror smiled back. "That was a narrow escape," they said. "We thought we had lost you forever."

Just as in C's poem, a door had opened.